Turning
Rocks
into
Diamonds

A Guide to Leading Leaders
Into the New Millennium

Turning Rocks Into Diamonds

Cynthia M. Thompson

XULON PRESS ELITE

Xulon Press
2301 Lucien Way #415
Maitland, FL 32751
407.339.4217
www.xulonpress.com

© 2019 by Cynthia M. Thompson

All rights reserved solely by the author. The author guarantees all contents are original and do not infringe upon the legal rights of any other person or work. No part of this book may be reproduced in any form without the permission of the author. The views expressed in this book are not necessarily those of the publisher.

Unless otherwise indicated, scripture quotations taken from the Amplified Bible (AMP). Copyright © 1954, 1958, 1962, 1964, 1965, 1987 by The Lockman Foundation. Used by permission. All rights reserved.

Printed in the United States of America.

ISBN-13: 978-1-6295-2963-9

Contents

Chapter 1	Loving Beyond Imperfections	1
Chapter 2	Natural vs. Spiritual Leadership	17
Chapter 3	Fledgling Leadership: Getting Your Feet Wet	35
Chapter 4	Domestic Leadership: Restoring the Family Focus	67
Chapter 5	The Fragrance of the Anointing: Is it Real or a Knock-off?	81
Bibliography		89

CHAPTER 1

LOVING BEYOND IMPERFECTIONS

During our years of ministry, we have had many people come into our ministry. Some have stayed the course, while others felt "led", and they jumped ship. One day in my frustration, I was talking to my spiritual leader to get some encouragement about dealing with people. He graciously expressed to me that we have to "love rocks until they become diamonds." After our conversation, I wrote that phrase on a post-it note and posted it at my desk. I looked at that phrase on that small, red piece of paper every day until it became a part of my heart.

When we are first placed in the ministry, we don't get a manual on how to correctly love God's people. Our love should represent the Father's love; however, when added all up, the love ends up being on the surface…superficial and conditional. In ministry, we, as leaders bump our heads so often, and in our ignorance run new converts or members away because our love can't see beyond their rough edges. In the natural, we attempt to raise our children the way our parents raised us, and this is carried over in the spiritual realm.

Coming from a strict background, we always tried to "clean the fish before we caught the fish." In early ministry, messages revolved around, "You have to do this…you can't do this…you can't do that." We put too much pressure on the rocks, causing them to disintegrate. These baby rocks walk away discouraged and without hope.

The adage, "never judge a book by its cover" still stands true today. To love rocks, one must not judge the inner potential by the rough, outer exterior that new converts present when they first enter the Body of Christ. Upon the start of our ministry, a young lady started attending our church. She was rough around the edges. She found it difficult to communicate with people without being harsh, almost biting their heads off with her responses. Some would get offended because of her communication problems to the point where no one wanted to work with her, but we continued to love this person along with her jagged edges. She has overcome so many struggles, and through the Word, many layers have fallen from her. She has overcome many obstacles and battles, and through it all, she began to take shape. The brilliance of the diamond within her began to shine through. The facets of her diamond has taken shape.

Rocks come in all different shapes, colors, and sizes. The three main categories that rocks fall into are sedimentary, metamorphic, or igneous. Rocks are used for various purposes whether as decorations or for barriers. Rocks have a cycle of life. Over some time, rocks become new rocks. Rocks have to go through tremendous heat and pressure before becoming diamonds. Not all rocks become diamonds, but those that are destined to be diamonds must go through a rigorous process.

When looking at the outward appearance of the rock, one will think that this hard, porous object has no inside potential. They don't realize there are facets of brilliancy within the inner core, but it must be developed. At the initial observation of the rock, the cost is determined as worthless; however, in the final observation of the diamond, the cost is priceless. In the Body of Christ, we as leaders are sometimes so quick to judge a person based on their outward appearance. We encourage our sons and daughters by telling them that they have potential, but we don't allow them the time to be developed for their potential to become reality. Development is a process that we all must go through. During the developmental stage, leaders must realize the stage that the person is in, and love them through the pressure, adversity, and struggle.

When considering the most important word of the phrase "loving rocks until they become diamonds," the word "love" is the driving force in this statement. The word "love" here is the Greek word *agape*. Love is greater than speaking in tongues, giving of ourselves, or any other great feat that we can accomplish in life. In today's vernacular, love is more lip service than from the heart. Leaders must learn how to love who God has entrusted to them with His love and not with man-made love.

> 1 Peter 4:7-8 (MSG)
> Everything in the world is about to be wrapped up, so take nothing for granted. Stay wide-awake in prayer. Most of all, love each other as if your life depended on it. Love makes up for practically anything.

> Romans 5:8, 10-11 (MSG)
> But God put his love on the line for us by offering his Son in sacrificial death while we were of no use whatever to him. If, when we were at our worst, we were put on friendly terms with God by the sacrificial death of his Son, now that we're at our best, just think of how our lives will expand and deepen by means of his resurrection life.

True love (God's love) covers a multitude of sins. St. John 3:16 shows us that for God so loved the world that He gave His only Son. God gave us His best, His only Son, when we were only rocks with no physical, outward appearance. Even when we were sinners, He yet loved us. So, what is our excuse when we don't love the ones that God has entrusted to us even in their imperfections?

Our salvation was based upon Jesus completing His mission so that we would not perish but have everlasting life. Jesus completed His mission through His life, death, and resurrection. Even to the death of the cross, through all the pain and humiliation that He had to suffer, He never forgot His mission. His mission was to redeem mankind and return us to the Father. They mocked and scorned Him, and even had the nerve to call Him everything except the Son of God, but yet He still fulfilled His mission. Even in the Garden of Gethsemane when Jesus wanted the Father to take the cup from Him, He (Jesus) made the final decision that it was not about His (Jesus') will, but the will of the Father. Leaders must take on the same Christ-like attitude. The mission must be fulfilled.

Leaders must learn obedience through the things they suffer from the ones that God has allowed to come in their part of the Body. It hurts leaders that the ones that they help out the most are the ones that hurt them the most; however, the mission still has to be accomplished. Leaders will be accused of many things. There will be some that will come into the fold masquerading as a rock. Their result will be that they will sink to the bottom of the ocean. There will be some rocks that will desire admiration and recognition and when they don't receive what they came for, they move to someone else's garden to be used as a decoration, only to be forgotten. Even though leaders will encounter the different forms of rocks, they must continue to love God's people regardless. Leaders must always be willing to forgive because if love is operating properly, God's love will cover the hurt and sin of the one that has done the leader wrong. God's love looks beyond man's fault and see their needs.

In I Corinthians 13, Paul describes God's love. If God's Word is applied to our lives and we practice what we are being taught, then leaders will have no problem moving from lip service to loving straight from the heart. The passage starts, "Though I speak with tongues of men and angels, and have not charity, I am become as sounding brass, or a tinkling cymbal." If our love is not right or we are not loving our little ones as we have been instructed, our tongues of praise, worship, and prayer language is noise unto God. If we are not operating in God's love toward His people, all the things that we assume we are doing before God is like a novice playing a drum set or someone scratching a chalkboard with their nails.

Love (*agape*) should be unconditional and fervent. Even on the cross, Jesus asked His Father to forgive the executioners and all those who put Him to death because He said they didn't realize what they were doing. Now, that is love to ask the Father to forgive those who just recently welcomed you into their city, but who suddenly turned their backs on you, and chose a murderer over you...an innocent man. Leaders must walk in true discipleship, and that is operating in God's love instead of our human love. If we are first and foremost Christians (followers of Christ), we are obligated to do what we have seen Him do. What did He do? He loved God's people regardless. When He told His Father, "It is finished," Jesus knew in His heart of hearts that His mission was fulfilled. Even on their worst day, His love for God's people did not change. Again, we, as leaders, must take on this same Christ-like attitude.

> 1 John 4:20-21 (MSG)
>
> If anyone boasts, "I love God," and goes right on hating his brother or sister, thinking nothing of it, he is a liar. If he won't love the person he can see, how can he love the God he can't see? The command we have from Christ is blunt: Loving God includes loving people. You've got to love both.

Secondly, 1 Corinthians 13 points out that we may flow prophetically, have a deep understanding of spiritual things, and even have faith to move mountains, but if we don't operate in love, to God we are nothing. Without love, we can't even give things to other people or charity, thinking that will do anything for us or make us big in His sight. He requires us to love His people no matter what. How can we stand before God's people, unfold mysteries of God's love, but can't stand God's people?

> 2 Timothy 2:24-26 (MSG)
> God's servant must not be argumentative, but a gentle listener and a teacher who keeps cool, working firmly but patiently with those who refuse to obey. You never know how or when God might sober them up with a change of heart and a turning to the truth, enabling them to escape the devil's trap, where they are caught and held captive, forced to run his errands.

Love or charity is described as patient. Once in position, leaders feel as though they don't have to be patient with people anymore. Some act as though they have arrived on some majestic pedestal forgetting that it is only by God's grace or they would be in the same places, making the wrong choices, and making the same mistakes. Have you ever heard of the familiar saying, "Patience is a virtue"? Patience, according to Merriam-Webster's Dictionary, comes from the root word "patient." It defines "patient" as "bearing pains or trials calmly or without complaint; manifesting forbearance under provocation or strain; not hasty or impetuous; steadfast despite opposition, difficulty, or adversity and able or willing to bear." Strong's Concordance backs the definition of "suffereth long" by the Greek word, makrothymeō, which means "to be of a long spirit, not to lose heart; to persevere patiently and bravely in enduring misfortunes and troubles; to be patient in bearing the offenses and injuries of others; to be mild and slow in avenging; to be longsuffering, slow to anger, slow to punish." As God has never given up on us, what gives us the right to give up on people?

> Proverbs 24:10 (MSG)
> If you fall to pieces in a crisis, there wasn't much to you in the first place.

When adversity comes, leaders tend to shrink back and lose heart. Many leaders have given up their assignment simply because they were faced with opposition or some type of difficulty. Leaders need to develop tough skin so that they can endure the unattractive seasons. Adverse conditions will fall upon every ministry, but leaders will be judged on their response to adversity.

During difficult times, leaders want to wear their feelings on their sleeve and have a deep desire to validate their right and avenge the wrong that has been done to them. Leaders must endure hardness as a good soldier. A good soldier is committed to stay until the end of the battle. Soldiers do not run during the heat of the battle, but they persevere through the tough times. They are brave and willing to lose their lives for the cause.

Leaders are God's generals, and the job of the general is to lead the troops through the battle to their victory. If the enemy can get the general to lose courage, then he can get the troops.

Don't give up your courage just because adversity has surfaced and is inviting you to retreat to the foxhole. Leaders must be steadfast (firmly fixed in place; not subject to change; firm in belief, determination, or adherence). Leaders want their followers to be loyal, but how can the followers be loyal to the cause if they see their leader not being loyal and running in the face of adversity?

> Colossians 3:12-14 (MSG)
> So, chosen by God for this new life of love, dress in the wardrobe God picked out for you: compassion, kindness, humility, quiet strength, discipline. Be

even-tempered, content with second place, quick to forgive an offense. Forgive as quickly and completely as the Master forgave you. And regardless of what else you put on, wear love. It's your basic, all-purpose garment. Never be without it.

Thirdly, love is kind. This is a quality that does not correlate with some of today's leaders. Some leaders are not kind to God's people thus hurting people deep in their hearts. This type of leader is of the attitude, "Because I said it, it is law." However, even if it is law, we must be careful about how we treat people. We must be gentle and handle the ones that God has entrusted to us with care. As rocks going through a metamorphosis, they are in a gentle state. Some will allow the hardness to drive them deeper into the earth's surface and go through the process, while others will roll away, not wanting to put up with the harsh treatment.

In Hebrews 12:13, we are instructed to "follow peace with all men." Kindness is a quality of which we can't get enough. Kindness will force you to treat individuals with equity and fairness. Kindness will make you, as a leader, treat your followers in the right way. In Proverbs, it encourages us that a "soft answer turns away wrath." What if we are not treated back with kindness? Eventually, we will reap our true harvest. We will reap exactly what we have sown. If we sow kindness, it is inevitable to reap kindness. Always remember God's Word cannot lie. He is faithful to His Word and promises.

Charity (love) envieth not. Leaders should not get to the place where they are jealous or envious as their people are going through the process. As God's people are being developed in their various roles, Christians tend to try their wings before time. Leaders cannot become envious because it appears the rock is developing a spiritual gift or insight that they don't have. Some leaders tend to downplay the gifts that are being poured upon their people if they don't operate in that gift. Instead of going to God and asking for understanding, they will attempt to shut this gift down, hurting the individual's feelings without realizing God is developing this rock into a diamond in that specific area. A spirit of jealousy or envy should never be in the heart of a leader.

In 1 Samuel 18, the Bible tells us that Saul operated in the spirit of jealousy against David. He was so jealous of David that he attempted to kill David numerous times. Saul could not continue to do the will of God because continual jealousy and disobedience took him out of God's will. Saul was so consumed with the words of the people and the accolades that David received that he forgot that they were on the same team.

The goal of the spiritual leader is to stretch their followers to exceed where they have been. What kind of parent does not want their children to have more than what they had?

Disobedience and jealousy cost Saul the throne. Many leaders are being dethroned simply because of their disobedience because they allow themselves to develop a spirit of jealousy within the heart. Instead of developing upcoming leaders to continue the work, many leaders get frightened and feel threatened that they allow envy to hinder the work from making forward progress.

There is no need to allow the spirit of jealousy to rear its ugly head when we should be cheering our upcoming leaders on to success. If we never reproduce and raise successors, our ministries will be stagnant, and we will be old and tired before our time. Leaders must allow the true love of God to eradicate the jealousy that attempts to crop up in their hearts from time to time.

> 1 Samuel 18:5-9 (MSG)
>
> Whatever Saul gave David to do, he did it well. So well that Saul put him in charge of his military operations. Everybody, both the people in general and Saul's servants, approved of and admired David's leadership. As they returned home, after David had killed the Philistine, the women poured out

of all the villages of Israel singing and dancing, welcoming King Saul with tambourines, festive songs, and lutes. In playful frolic the women sang, "Saul kills by the thousand, David by the ten thousand!" This made Saul angry—very angry. He took it as a personal insult. He said, "They credit David with 'ten thousand and me with only 'thousands.' Before you know it, they'll be giving him the kingdom!" From that moment on, Saul kept his eye on David.

Spiritual leaders need to have mirror time to deal with their insecurities. In taking the time for self-examination, when the spirit of jealousy attempts to crop up, it must be immediately dealt with and crushed. Thus, the spiritual leader is enabled to flow in their proper place while encouraging their members to grow and excel in the things of God.

During our season of leadership, we must not allow the "Saul spirit" to crop up in our hearts because this will cause us to lose the precious anointing that God imparted within us.

God looked beyond our every fault and saw our need. It is our duty and responsibility to love those entrusted to us beyond their fault. If our love is right, even though the imperfection is there, it will not affect or change how we deal with the person. There are so many days, that even in our sanctified selves, we mess up, but God does not throw us away or count us unworthy. Even on our worst day, His love for us does not change. Remember at one time, we were where they are. Do not forget where you came from, and act as though you have arrived and are perfected in all areas. We have brilliant facets emerging but there are still some areas in our lives that are still being perfected. Always remember that we are all works in progress. We must love our spiritual children with the heat of God's love that is within us until it melts the stony hardness of their exterior and reveals the brilliant facets that are locked within them.

CHAPTER 2

NATURAL VS. SPIRITUAL LEADERSHIP

"The very essence of leadership is that you have to have vision. You can't blow an uncertain trumpet."
– Theodore M. Hesburgh

"If you have to tell people that you're a leader, you are probably not."
–Author Unknown

Some people have natural-born leadership traits, while others, through experience, have developed certain traits along the way. There are even some people that consider themselves to be leaders but are not leaders at all. It does not matter if a person has natural-born leadership traits or not—they need training and mentorship to help develop and pull these traits out of them. To become an effective leader, one must first be an effective follower.

> Proverbs 29:18 (KJV)
> Where there is no vision, the people perish: but he that keepeth the law, happy is he.

To be a natural or a spiritual leader, you must first have a vision. Webster defines "vision" as "the formation of a mental image of something that is not perceived as real and is not present to the senses." How can you lead or make an effective change without first having a vision for your organization? Many organizations and churches go awry because the person who is assigned to be the visionary does not know how to lead the people. This is clearly why the Lord instructed Habakkuk to write the vision clearly so the people could see the plan of action.

> Habakkuk 2:2 (AMP)
> And the Lord answered me and said, "Write the vision and engrave it so plainly upon tablets that everyone who

passes may [be able to] read [it easily and quickly] as he hastens by."

Vision is important to any organization. Without a vision, a mission cannot be clearly defined, thus leaving the followers with minimal or no direction. In addition to vision, natural leaders must be creative, innovative, and not afraid to take risks. Natural leaders must possess the skill to give their subordinates a clear picture instead of a knothole view.

A natural leader is one who is self-confident in his ambitions and has the initiative to get things moving. They set high goals for themselves and are not outwardly afraid to accomplish these goals. A natural leader will get the job done regardless of who they have to step on to get it done. Their bossy attitude will enable them to give commands with the expectation that the job will be completed to their satisfaction. They are not passive and will be assertive enough to always make themselves "shine." They are passionate about what they believe in and can sometimes be outspoken.

When God created natural leaders, he placed something special within them. However, as people begin to notice these characteristics, the person begins to think it is all about them. They don't depend on God for guidance in their decision-making process but have complete reliance on themselves that they are on the right track. They are highly confident in their efforts because they will say, "See what I did," or, "It would not have got done if I..." They carry so many traits that are tied around their performance that they fail to realize it was a team effort. Natural leaders usually stand a notch above everyone else, and their efforts are recognized. They only feel accountable to the carrying out of the mission. They thrive on recognition and achievement. A natural leader with a vision can pull people together to work together for one common cause.

In experience, I have had the opportunity of working with good leaders and some that were not so good. Some managers encouraged, mentored, and pulled the best out of employees. However, other managers were threatened by employees' knowledge, skills, and abilities. Instead of capitalizing on these qualities, the leaders downplayed these qualities, thus causing the employee to lose motivation.

In my professional life, there is one great manager (leader) who comes to mind. He was such a motivator. He was helpful and understanding. He encouraged me to go back to school to get my degree. As a result of his encouragement and motivation, today I hold an Associate's, a Bachelors', and two Master's degrees. He had a vision for our department, and instead of him beating us up to get the work done, he worked alongside us to get the mission fulfilled. He was loved and respected by not only those who worked with him, but he was respected by those who worked under him. He inspired us to be team players with a "can-do" attitude. He was a soft-spoken man, but he had tact for pointing the way. He was a quiet giant in his own right.

WHAT IS SPIRITUAL LEADERSHIP?

Spiritual leadership is similar to natural leadership. Both forms originate from God and the traits need to be developed within an individual. However, spiritual leadership goes a little deeper than that of someone performing duties as a natural leader.

In David Reid's article entitled, "Spiritual Leadership", he defines spiritual leadership as "God-given ability and responsibility to lead God's people." This all-important dimension is a "must" for effective leadership in any Christian service. As in the case of the natural leader, a spiritual leader must have a vision. A spiritual leader must be innovative and creative as they are making their vision known to their followers. However, a natural leader can operate naturally, but a spiritual leader must fully rely on God.

In another one of Reid's articles entitled, "Devotions for Growing Christians", he explains:

> There are certain elements common to all types of leadership. Furthermore, the good qualities of military leadership, political leadership or corporate leadership can certainly be used by the Lord

when a committed Christian dedicates these natural and developed abilities to Christ. Spiritual leadership, however, is more than just dedicated natural traits and talents.

THE SPIRIT OF HUMILITY

The first characteristic a spiritual leader must possess is humility. He must first be a servant. If a follower does not want to do a menial task because of fear that they will not get recognized or promoted, they are not ready to be a leader. A spiritual leader must be a servant first. A spiritual leader must be willing to sacrifice his life for the comfort of others. The work that a spiritual leader does is not attributed to his or her natural talents or abilities.

The path to being blessed is that we must be a servant just like Jesus was. There was nothing beneath Him—even when he washed Peter's feet (John 13:3-16). We should never get to the point where we forget our real purpose of being a leader, and that is to serve those who are entrusted to us. As outlined in an article entitled "Characteristics of Christian Leadership" the author explains servant leadership is other-centered, not self-centered, and is God-honoring. He goes on to say:

> The servant-leader is not preoccupied with what they gain from leadership.

They are not interested in status or comfort. They willingly undergo hardship and suffering humbling themselves to meet the needs of others. They are not too important or dignified to undertake even the lowest of tasks and they do so with no thought of personal gain.

When operating in humility, leaders will be subjected to some unpleasantness before they receive honor. Being a spiritual leader is not about the glitz, glamour, and having your name in lights, but taking the low road, loving God's people in spite of your hurt, and maintaining a servant's heart. David Reagan explains in his article, "A Servant's Heart" that:

> Biblical humility is the opposite of selfishness; it is selflessness. It is not a hatred of self or an embarrassment of self. It is a removing of self from conscious thought. It is a life so lost in pleasing God that there is no time and no need to please self. Pleasing God brings satisfaction. Humility is not a heightened sense of self and a hatred of that self. It is a losing of self in God and in others. God is all and in all. This is a servant's heart. This is the disciple's calling.

Spiritual leaders must avoid the temptation to become haughty because the result will be humiliation. Reagan goes on to explain:

> A disciple can either exalt himself (haughtiness) or he can humble himself (humility). As a result, he will either be abased (humiliation) or he will be exalted (honor). This principle goes totally against the practice of the world where a man must promote himself in order to gain position.

It should be the goal of each leader to be more self-effacing rather than self-promoting. We should not be bringing attention to ourselves, but point the attention back to God, thus giving Him all the glory. Humility is such an important asset that spiritual leaders must possess because if not, they are on a road toward destruction. We were given a choice to either remain humble and receive our exaltation from God or exalt ourselves and receive our humiliation from God.

> John 3:30
> He must increase, but I must decrease.

We must do our assignments from a servant's perspective, thus leading us to the next point.

> Mark 10:42-45
> So Jesus called them together and said, "You know that in this world kings are tyrants, and officials lord it over the people beneath them. But among you it should be quite different. Whoever wants to be a leader among you must be your servant, and whoever wants to be first must be the slave of all. For even I, the Son of Man, came here not to be served but to serve others, and to give my life as a ransom for many."

A SERVANT'S HEART

If Jesus didn't come to be served, but to serve others, what is our excuse for not wanting to serve? A spiritual leader is responsible for those who are entrusted to their care, and they have to love and nurture them. A spiritual leader has the God-given obligation to lead by example. If followers see the leaders serving, they will have no problem with serving. However, when they see the leader barking orders but not willing to get his or her hands dirty, followers get a bad attitude and begin to resist the leader. A spiritual leader should not possess a mean spirit, but they should be willing to love God's people regardless. As leaders, our God-given obligation to the assignment is to lead, feed, and oversee, but how are we carrying out our assignment? Our love for God's people must be genuine, and we must be enthusiastic regarding our calling. If we aren't eager, God's people will surely know, and they will not be apt to follow a leader who does not want to be in position.

> 1 Peter 5:2-3
> Care for the flock of God entrusted to you. Watch over it willingly, not grudgingly—not for what you will get out of it, but because you are eager to serve God. Don't lord it over the people assigned to your care, but lead them by your good example.

A good example is important because it establishes trust between the leader and the follower. If the people see the leader has integrity, they feel more comfortable allowing that specific leader to take them to the next level and dimension. The problem is that in these last days, many spiritual leaders have failed, thus leaving their followers in a thick cloud of despair and disappointment. Lord, help us to complete our assignment with integrity and honesty before God's people. As spiritual leaders, this should be our prayer at the end of every day. There is no time for spiritual leaders to lead double lives with double tongues. In today's society, people are looking for someone stable, one who will not allow himself to bend when adversities come along.

In today's society, we must consider the forerunners as our examples as we lead God's people. If we would use the Godly examples of Paul, Peter, and even Jesus instead of being legends in our mind, I am persuaded spiritual leaders wouldn't bump their heads as much making a mess over their flock.

As spiritual leaders, the important word in this phrase is "spiritual." As Paul admonished the Romans to present their bodies "as a living sacrifice, holy, acceptable unto God which is your reasonable service", the same applies to us. We should keep this in the forefront of our minds and hearts. We can't expect our followers to lead a clean, holy life if we, as leaders, are not exemplifying this life before them. "Like priests, like people," we can't stand on God's holy platform spewing out mere words without actions that correspond to these words.

Spiritual leaders must have their relationship with the Lord Jesus Christ. One of the priorities is being knowledgeable in the Word of God. It is vital that as a spiritual leader, we must keep our sword sharp at all times. Our heart must be attentive to the study of God's Word. God has chosen spiritual leaders after His own heart to feed their followers with knowledge and understanding. How can spiritual leaders feed God's flock with knowledge and understanding if they are not well-versed in the Word of God?

We should exhaust ourselves in the Word of God, pulling out the nuggets of truth. It is a great disservice to God's people to either try to feed them warmed-over or leftover meals. It is our responsibility to give our flock fresh, green grass every time that they are assembled in our presence. As the adage goes, "The grass is greener on the other side. This can be true if all we do is give our sheep brown, dried-up hay. God fed His people (the Israelites) fresh manna daily. He expects the same for the leaders that He has set up before His people today. Most importantly, leaders should not only be students of the Word of God but must be doers of the Word of God, leading by example.

> Prayer is the vital breath of the Christian, not the thing that makes him alive, but the evidence that he is alive. – Oswald Chambers

> Prayer breaks all bars, dissolves all chains, opens all prisons, and widens all straits by which God's saints have been held. – EM Bounds

A PRODUCTIVE PRAYER LIFE

Another characteristic that a spiritual leader must possess is having a productive prayer life. Leaders need to get back to praying fervently for themselves and their flocks. Many leaders are fainting because their prayer life is minimal. Without prayer, many leaders are operating on fumes. After pouring out before God's people, leaders must go back in prayer for a refueling. For instance, a car does not run off of the same tank of gas from the time you drive it off of the dealership's parking lot to the time it becomes a clunker. Periodically, you have to stop to get fuel. At times, the car breaks down and requires maintenance (oil change, new plugs, wires, new tires, so on and so forth). The same applies to leaders; however, because of title or elevation, some leaders get to the place where they feel as they have arrived, and they are the best thing since sliced bread.

Even after Jesus did miracles, He went back to a solitary place and talked to His Father. What was He doing? He was refueling and getting ready for His next assignment. Instead of refueling with our Father, we end up in restaurants and other venues catering to our natural man, when our depleted spirit man is the one that requires special attention.

Our prayers need to be effective and they should get the job done. The flock that is entrusted to the leader should be his or her focus when praying. It should be a daily prayer to God that He will show the leader how to effectively lead the people. The needs of the flock should be the needs of the leader. The leader should act as an intercessor between God and the people. They should not rest until their flock's needs are met. The leader should feel the pain of the sheep. As James 5:16 states, "the effectual, fervent prayer of the righteous availeth much."

> James 5:16-18 (MSG)
>
> Make this your common practice: Confess your sins to each other and pray for each other so that you can live together whole and healed. The prayer of a person living right with God is something powerful to be reckoned with. Elijah, for instance, human just like us, prayed hard that it wouldn't rain, and it didn't—not a drop for three and a half years. Then he prayed that it would

rain, and it did. The showers came and everything started growing again.

Spiritual leaders must get to a place where they carry a burden for God's people. What great parents are those who never feel the hurt of their children? They are not great at all. They are insensitive and have not died out to their selfish desires. A shepherd who possesses a genuine love for his sheep will put his life on the line to save his sheep. He will forget about his safety just to save one of his little ones.

Thus, equating this to a spiritual leader, it is not about saving face, but we have to do what needs to be done to not allow the wolf to come in and devour our sheep even to our hurt. We will have to give account for each sheep, so it is to our advantage to be watchful, alert, and prayerful at all times.

> Matthew 18:12-13 (MSG)
> Look at it this way. If someone has a hundred sheep and one of them wanders off, doesn't he leave the ninety-nine and go after the one? And if he finds it, doesn't he make far more over it than over the ninety-nine who stay put?

Spiritual leaders learn how to deal with people. As the leader, you must be persuasive enough to motivate, not manipulate, your flock to follow through. You must learn to be a people person. Reid points out in his article "Spiritual Leadership: Devotions for Growing Christians" that Ezra knew how to work well with people. Ezra had to convince the Levites who grew accustomed to the easy Babylonian life to return back to Jerusalem. The result is that Ezra managed to motivate approximately 250 Levites to return to the work of the Lord (Ezra 8:15). It is the job of the spiritual leader to be the motivator of the flock so that they will not become complacent in their duties. The shepherd must guide the flock of sheep to the desired destination.

Reid also points out that Ezra possessed a "flexible firmness" when working with people. The article goes on to say, "When Ezra was confronted with a moral problem on the part of God's people (Ezra 9:1-4), he didn't condone sin or change God's standards to water down the problem."

No matter how close we get to our flock, we can never take on the smell of our flock. We must not compromise God's standards just to keep the flock happy. However, we have to be "minute managers." Minute managers are managers that take care of the issue and move on. We always have to maintain an attitude of flexibility. We don't have a right to demand anything. We have to always be apt to listen and hear the whole matter before drawing any conclusions.

Spiritual leaders must also be wise in the handling of God's money. It is not wise for a spiritual leader to always count or handle the money. However, always remember the church is a business, and you must know what is going on in the back office. Embezzlement and mismanagement of funds can happen right under your nose, and if you are not aware of the accounts, you will never know it until it is too late. As Reid points out, "A balanced approach to finances is a mark of a good spiritual leader."

CHAPTER 3

FLEDGLING LEADERSHIP: GETTING YOUR FEET WET

1 Timothy 1:12 (AMP)
I give thanks to Him Who has granted me [the needed] strength and made me able [for this], Christ Jesus our Lord, because He has judged and counted me faithful and trustworthy, appointing me to [this stewardship of] the ministry.

Congratulations on making the first step in the ministry. How awesome it is to be entrusted to such an awesome work. God could have picked anyone, but He selected *you!* You will experience many things as you embark on this exciting adventure. How I wish that I had this chapter when we first started in ministry.

It would have saved much heartache along the way. Being chosen for the work of the ministry is such an honor. It is an intimidating transition from follower to leader, but the Bible teaches us to walk and live by faith and not by sight (2 Corinthians 5:7).

We are made able and competent through Christ Jesus. When I heard this amazing revelation, it humbled me to learn I had been judged and counted faithful and trustworthy by Christ Jesus to the work of the ministry. Being in the ministry was something that I never aspired. This was a step that I initially did not want to take. The responsibilities were too great because I thought it was about me and my strengths, talents, and abilities.

We can no longer make excuses because of our inadequacies because it is God who has equipped us to do the work at hand. We simply have to trust Him. We have a job to do and if we continue to make excuses, we are not going to bring glory to God. Time does not wait for anyone, so it is up to us to do what God has called us to do.

From our mother's womb, the decree of the King was made that we would bring Him delight and pleasure through our work in the ministry. Once the decree goes out, it is sealed and is a done deal. We have been handpicked. We have to go where God tells us to go, and do what He tells us to do regardless of what others think of or do to us. God has equipped us and put His words in our mouths. It is up to us to open our mouths and speak what God has told us to speak. We cannot suffer from the Jeremiah syndrome, thinking we are inadequate for the assignment because of our stature, age, or anything else that could hold us back from accomplishment. We see at the beginning of Jeremiah's call, he made excuses because he thought he was too young and he didn't know anything.

But this is what God said:

> "Before I shaped you in the womb, I knew all about you. Before you saw the light of day, I had holy plans for you: A prophet to the nations—that's what I had in mind for you." But I said, "Hold it, Master God! Look at me. I don't know anything. I'm only a boy!" God told me, "Don't say, 'I'm only a boy.' I'll tell you where to go and you'll go there. I'll tell you what to say and you'll say it. Don't be afraid of a soul. I'll be right there, looking after you." God's Decree. God reached out, touched my mouth, and said, "Look! I've just put my words in your mouth—hand-delivered! See what I've done? I've given you a job to do among nations and governments—a red-letter day! Your job is to pull up and tear down, take apart and

> demolish, and then start over, building and planting."
> Jeremiah 1:5-10 (MSG)

Also, we find that Moses suffered from a speech impediment and he made an excuse regarding it. He thought this might get him out of his assignment, but not so. God knows who He wants and He knows what He is doing.

> Exodus 4:10-13 (NIV)
> Moses said to the Lord, "O Lord, I have never been eloquent, neither in the past nor since you have spoken to your servant. I am slow of speech and tongue." The Lord said to him, "Who gave man his mouth? Who makes him deaf or mute? Who gives him sight or makes him blind? Is it not I, the Lord? Now go; I will help you speak and will teach you what to say." But Moses said, "O Lord, please send someone else to do it."

We gladly sing the song, "Lord, I'll go, Lord, I'll go … If the Lord needs somebody, here am I, oh, Lord, send me." How ironic that when He comes looking for us to send us, we suggest to Him to send someone else to do the job? We find that even after God told Moses that He would help him speak and God offered to teach Moses what to say, that was not enough reassurance for him. Therefore, Moses dared to ask the Lord to send someone else.

No one else can perform the assignment that has been tailor-made for you. As we go on to read:

> (Exodus 4:14-17, NIV)
> Then the Lord's anger burned against Moses and he said, "What about your brother, Aaron the Levite? I know he can speak well. He is already on his way to meet you, and his heart will be glad when he sees you. You shall speak to him and put words in his mouth; I will help both of you speak and will teach you what to do. He will speak to the people for you, and it will be as if he were your mouth and as if you were God to him. But take this staff in your hand so you can perform miraculous signs with it."

God got angry with Moses, but that did not change His mind regarding the appointment. God, in His infinite wisdom, still raised up Moses to lead the children of Israel, but Aaron just spoke the words that God instructed Moses to say. However, we find that God gave Moses the staff in his hand (he was the shepherd of the flock), and this was used to perform the miracles that confirmed the words that were spoken from God.

Our assignments will not be based solely on our natural ability, but it will take our availability to get the task done. As we begin in ministry, we have to realize that our assignments will not be completed in our natural strength, but it will be God doing the work through us. At the end of the day, our main goal is to ensure we have brought God pleasure and delight in all that we do, whether we are ministering to God's people or conducting ministerial business.

As you are beginning in ministry, always remember your true identity. It should not be your goal to take on someone else's mannerisms but be comfortable in your anointing. Remember you have been granted the needed strength to take on this assignment. It is Jesus Christ our Lord who has enabled us for the ministry. This mission is more than just preaching, but at the end of the day, it is about loving God's people. You have been appointed and anointed by not only the presbyteries but by God Himself. Your obligation is to Him first, and then to His people. Sometimes, you will feel as you cannot make it another step, but keep in the forefront of your mind that you have been granted the needed strength to make the next step.

> Philippians 2:13 (AMP)
> [Not in your own strength] for it is God Who is all the while effectually at work in you [energizing and creating in you the power and desire], both to will and to work for His good pleasure and satisfaction and] delight.

God is effectually at work in us. His Word is operative and is put forth in power through us. It is He who is giving us the power, the drive, and the desire to do what needs to be done in the ministry. We have to realize God is the audience, and we need to do our best that we move Him. Our charisma can be used to move people while God is not moved at all. It is time that we move God. How exciting it would be to get a standing ovation from God! What a humbling experience it will be to hear, "Job well done" from God Himself.

> Matthew 25:21 (AMP)
> His master said to him, "Well done, you upright (honorable, admirable) and faithful servant! You have been faithful and trustworthy over a little; I will put

you in charge of much. Enter into and share the joy (the delight, the blessedness) which your master enjoys."

Now that you have decided to accept God's call, as a new leader, there are things that you need to know. To "launch out in the deep," you must first get your feet wet by jumping in the pool. However, when a person is taught to swim, they are not thrown into the ten-foot section. First, the instructor tries to help the student gain confidence by overcoming their fear of the water; thus, the purpose of this manual.

You will be a strong leader. It will not happen overnight, but with much practice, you will be leading with much finesse and confidence.

Throughout our journey in the ministry, these are some of the lessons learned.

> 1 Corinthians 4:14-16 (MSG)
> I'm not writing all this as a neighborhood scold just to make you feel rotten. I'm writing as a father to you, my children. I love you and want you to grow up well, not spoiled. There are a lot of people around who can't wait to tell you what you've done wrong, but there aren't many fathers willing to take the

time and effort to help you grow up. It was as Jesus helped me proclaim God's Message to you that I became your father. I'm not, you know, asking you to do anything I'm not already doing myself.

Pray to God for spiritual parents. During about our fourth year in ministry, one night I was watching a show on TBN. It was a Father's Day special on the importance of having spiritual parents. Then, my husband did not have an active spiritual father in his life, and I knew he longed for someone that he could confide in, and get ministerial advice.

I cried out to the Lord, and he answered my cry. He not only sent us a mentor but a "seer." Our lives and ministry have not been the same since we have submitted to our spiritual parents. Mentors are fine, but spiritual parents are necessary for proper growth. Spiritual parents are placed in our lives to correct and guide us on our way through this road called "ministry." Spiritual parents are needed to grow us. They are not there to be our best bosom buddies. They are in place to sternly correct when necessary, and then love on us and kiss our "boo-boos" when we mess up. There are many mentors but spiritual parents that have your best interests at heart are ordained by God.

If you need spiritual parents, simply pray and ask God. He will give you exactly who He has ordained for this very purpose. However, when He sends them your way, accept them. They might not be packaged based upon your wants, but they will be packaged according to your needs.

Spiritual parents will be your brakes when you are accelerating too fast, and in turn, they will be your accelerator when you are slowing down, holding up traffic. They will help you maintain your proper speed so you will not violate ruining your destiny.

Realize God will put spiritual parents in our lives who will be able to speak the very things that will unlock our potential that will lead us to our planned destiny. Always be open enough to hear what they have to say. Be ready to hear the words, "No, not right now." Remember, they see the bigger picture when we are looking at it from a knothole perspective.

Likewise, sometimes we are so close to the forest that we can't see the trees. We are so encapsulated in what we are doing that we don't always see the whole outcome. We need to seek and take heed to our spiritual parents' wise counsel because they have been where we are, and they can give us the right answers. Why try to pave a new road? Why do we have to always learn from our own mistakes when we can learn from the mistakes that our spiritual leaders made and were open enough to share with us? We don't have to be the martyr and suffer needlessly when we have spiritual parents that tell us not to go down that particular road but take the detour. As leaders, we are to be mindful that we are never above instruction or correction.

HAVE A GENUINE PASSION FOR WHAT YOU HAVE BEEN CALLED TO DO

> "Competence goes beyond words. It's the leader's ability to say it, plan it, and do it in such a way that others know that you know how — and know that they want to follow you." – John C. Maxwell

Loving what you do will emanate from your very being. How can you sell others on the vision if you are not fully persuaded yourself? "Passion" is defined in Webster's dictionary as "a strong liking or desire for or devotion to some activity, object, or concept." We have to love what we do at all times. The members that God blesses us with will be able to tell if the passion is there or not. We should have the attitude, "Come hell or high water, I will not falter or give up, but I am going to do God's will. It doesn't matter who comes or goes — I have an assignment from God and I am determined that this ministry will be fruitful."

Excitement is contagious. If the leader is excited about the vision, the people will catch the excitement.

It will spread throughout the congregation like wildfire. As the apostles in Acts turned the city upside down, our congregations will do the same thing.

When you have a passion for something, you will be excited about it. You will be so exuberant that you will shout from the rooftop, and if your members are excited about their church, they will shout and share with others. In turn, others will be drawn to your church to see what the buzz and excitement are all about.

Don't despise your beginnings. Whether you start in your house or a storefront facility with only your family members, don't despise your beginnings. You have to start somewhere. Everyone is not going to inherit a large congregation, but it is the leader's responsibility to grow the sheep that God entrusted to your care. Just be faithful in the least. When you start your ministry, start it with the spirit of excellence. Clean with excellence, decorate with excellence, administrate with excellence, and of course, teach and preach with excellence. Don't complain within yourself because it feels as if you are doing it all yourself. As my spiritual parents have taught us, "Maximize yourself on the level you are on and the next level will invite or pull you up."

Zechariah 4:10a (NLT)
Do not despise these small beginnings, for the Lord rejoices to see the work begin.

Not everyone will be supportive, and they will attempt to criticize you when you start; however, don't let anyone deter you from doing what God has established in your heart.

When we first came into ministry, we had fellow ministers ask us, "What do you think you are doing?" In other words, they were not happy about us starting a ministry, nor had they supported us in our journey. They were threatened by our presence and thought we were attempting to invade their turf or take their members. Fortunately, we did not allow this to deter us or stop us. It has placed a greater determination within us to do the work of the Lord.

You are in your part of the region for a reason. God does not do anything by chance or coincidence. There are some lives that only you can touch. Do your assignment and stay focused. Don't look to the left or right, but keep looking straight unto the hill from where your help comes.

God instructed Joshua to only be strong and of good courage. In ministry, only the strong will survive. Don't hold onto people, but hold onto the Word of God, because at the end of the day, only the Word will stand forever. Hold onto the instruction of your spiritual parents and those whom you have served in the ministry to be successful.

> Joshua 1:7 (NLT)
> Be strong and very courageous. Be careful to obey all the instructions Moses gave you. Do not deviate from them, turning either to the right or to the left. Then you will be successful in everything you do.

Be comfortable in who you are. We are all members of one body, the Body of Christ. We all have a specific function. We can't function as the eye when we have been destined to be the ear. On our natural body, our ear is designed to hear. If the ear begins to see, there will be a functionality problem. How will a normal person be able to see from the side of their head? We can't; we were not programmed that way.

Also, how can a person hear from the front of the head? The same: we were not programmed that way. We need to flow in the way that we are programmed. If we choose to flow and function against the way we have been designed, we are out of order and go in the wrong direction.

You don't need to be anyone else to be able to attract, impress, or motivate someone else. Can you imagine how these people will feel when they find out that you have been an imposter all along? In all that you do, always be genuine and real.

Be the example. Your message is only as effective as the life of the messenger. Many are turned off by ministry because the leader does the opposite of what they are teaching the members to do. At times, leaders can suffer from the "Do as I say, not as I do" syndrome. Never be accused of being a hypocrite. Always be true to your message.

Avoid familiarity. Have you ever heard the saying, "Familiarity breeds contempt"? From the beginning of your ministry, please let me stress to you, be careful who you allow in your inner circle. Even Jesus did not let all that walked with Him in His inner circle. He only let a few of his closest disciples to walk with Him. We see in the Garden of Gethsemane that He didn't even take all of His disciples with Him in His most desperate hour. The ones He took with Him could not even stay awake and pray with Him.

There will be people that will "hop" in your ministry because it is the new thing on the block. Their main assignment will be to get next to you. Some of those who will try to attach themselves to you will be strength-suckers. Because of their warped mentality and because they have so many visions that they can't see clearly, they will attempt to get next to you to get your secrets and steal your strength. Our enemy, Satan, is not happy because you started a ministry. You are an added threat to his kingdom and he will try to form weapons of mass destruction. How clever of him to use those who get the closest to us. For this purpose, we must stay prayerful and full of the Word of God so that we can be fully aware of the stratagem of our enemy.

> 2 Corinthians 2:11 (AMP)
> To keep Satan from getting the advantage over us; for we are not ignorant of his wiles and intentions.

God has placed tremendous love within us that will sometimes cause us to be vulnerable to the hurt of others. Don't let the wounds that others inflict upon you cause you to become bitter. When people become too familiar, they have studied you and know what makes you tick. Familiarity will cause them to lose respect for you because they will think that they are on the same level, and will expect to share the same pedestal. If you are not careful, they will knock you off of the pedestal, and they will.

Leadership is influence, whether good or bad. There will be people who will become members of your congregation who will have great influence. These are the ones that you need to watch because they can either make or break the vision that God has given you. These are the ones that will affect the followers. If left unattended, thinking they will go away, eventually they will gain enough power to split your church. Instead of ignoring their presence, divert their negative influence into a positive influence. As the saying goes, "keep your friends close but your enemies closer". Don't get so close to others that you are unable to see them plotting and scheming right under your nose. Don't override the discerning spirit that has been placed inside of you.

COUNT YOUR COSTS

> Proverbs 24:2-3 (Living Bible)
> Any enterprise is built by wise planning, becomes strong through common sense and profits wonderfully by keeping abreast of the facts.

It is never wise to jump into any venture with "rose-colored" glasses. It is advantageous to go in knowing all of the facts. Wise planning is the key to running your church and implementing your vision effectively. Throwing something together half-cocked has never been a great idea, and it will hurt you, your church, and its members in the long run. Counting your costs will save a lot of frustration and disappointment.

We find ourselves having book knowledge through everything we have learned in Bible College and seminary, but even after all of that, we find ourselves not using our God-given common sense. We have to have a vision that is well thought out and planned. How can a leader be effective when they have not carefully put their plan together? This is why so many leaders flounder and never get to the next level in their ministries and destiny.

Effective planning helps one to stay abreast of the facts. When facts are present, people are not apt to follow their emotions. Many churches are bankrupt and without members today because of the lack of wise planning and common sense. It takes common sense when dealing with people. We have to deal with them on their level. Some are simply not ready for Strong's and exegesis. They simply need to know someone loves and cares about them enough to take time out for them.

Without properly counting the costs, it brings on frustration and embarrassment. Do not take on something that you cannot finish. There will be naysayers waiting for the opportunity to chime in to say they knew it wasn't anything to what you were trying to do anyway.

> Luke 14:28-30 (MSG)
> Is there anyone here who, planning to build a new house, doesn't first sit down and figure the cost so you'll know if you can complete it? If you only get

the foundation laid and then run out of money, you're going to look pretty foolish. Everyone passing by will poke fun at you: 'He started something he couldn't finish.

With proper planning, common sense, and keeping abreast of the facts at hand, you will give them something to talk about—the good that your ministry is doing in the community. Wise planning and consistently keeping abreast of the facts will place longevity into the enterprise (your ministry). Counting the costs by using wise planning, common sense, and being abreast of the facts will promote profit and growth.

Treat others above how you want to be treated. This has been the mantra of our ministry. It should be your goal to treat others with dignity and respect. It is not based on their title or role they play within the church. All should be treated equally. Jesus loves us all the same, and so should we. We should not have partiality or be a respecter of persons. Many people have left churches simply because of blatant favoritism.

We will not be held responsible for how someone treats us, but we will be held accountable for how we respond to the treatment. I heard Shirley Caesar say in an interview and it has become a part of my spirit, "Do not allow anything to come between my soul and my Savior." We have to be apt to forgive and move on. We should not hold grudges but continue to treat others with dignity and respect. The Bible tells us that we should be kind one to another.

> Ephesians 4:32 (AMP)
> And become useful and helpful and kind to one another, tenderhearted (compassionate, understanding, loving-hearted), forgiving one another [readily and freely], as God in Christ forgave you.

Remember the law of sowing and reaping. When others are treated with dignity, fairness, and respect, dignity, fairness, and respect is reciprocated. Just because God has appointed you as the leader does not give you a right to lord that over anyone.

Many people leave churches because they feel as though they have been abused because of the harshness of the leader. In the natural, we shudder to think of abusing our children. We must apply the same principles to our role with our spiritual children. In today's society, parents are being severely prosecuted for abuse and neglect of their children. How are we going to escape the judgment of God if we neglect and abuse our spiritual children? Just as our natural children have been loaned to us, our spiritual children are on loan as well. We have to nurture, feed, and lead them to their God-given destiny.

It is against the nature of a mother to put her newborn infant in the crib, never attending to its needs but goes on about her business. You don't see this scenario too often. But in cases such as this, the Department of Social Services or Child Protective Services would come in and take the infant from the home. However, a mother carefully nurtures, feeds, and takes care of her baby until it reaches full adulthood.

I remember when I brought my newborns home from the hospital. I was so nervous that I did not even let them sleep in their room for several months. Even though the bassinet was next to my bed, I would still get up during the night to ensure that they were breathing properly.

At the strangest sound or cry, a mother will be on her feet to see what is wrong. Even to this day, I am still nervous if I hear a strange sound from one of my children's rooms. That is the love that a mother has for her children. Even if my children have done something to disappoint me or even make me angry, my love for them overrides what they have done. Therefore, if they are hurting, the love that I have for them causes me to run to their rescue.

Make it a point to study. We, as leaders, (fledgling or seasoned) must always make it a point to study. There are so many nuggets in God's Word that we don't get it all in one session. It is such a disservice to

God's people when leaders take the holy pulpit only to feed their spiritual children with a cold, stale, irrelevant word. Strong's definition of "study" is "to exert one's self, endeavor, give diligence." This is more than just picking up scripture and running with it. We must exert ourselves until we get the whole conclusion of the matter. It should be our goal to always provide and prepare a fresh message. In the natural, most people only eat leftovers for a couple of days; however, you don't find a person eating that stale, moldy dish three weeks later. It is thrown out.

> 2 Timothy 2:15 (AMP)
> Study and be eager and do your utmost to present yourself to God approved (tested by trial), a workman who has no cause to be ashamed, correctly analyzing and accurately dividing [rightly handling and skillfully teaching] the Word of Truth.

Remain prayerful and thankful. The Bible teaches us so much about prayer. The main degree that one must obtain to be effective in ministry is a degree in "kneeology." There will be things that you will not be able to share with anyone except God. There will be times that you will experience hurt so bad that you will not have the words to express to humans, but God understands the tears. Prayer is the key that keeps you built up when you want to give up. Do not ever stop communicating with God. If this happens, you will be disconnecting yourself from the Source. The Source is where the power is drawn. What good is an electrical appliance if it is unplugged from the source? The same applies to us and God. Never, ever lose your connection.

Always have a heart of thankfulness, no matter what. God will perfect all that concerns you. It is the will of the Father that we are always thankful. I am so blessed when my children (natural or spiritual) just say, "Thank you." It is so nice to be appreciated, and never take anyone for granted. If you have great staff, let them know how much you appreciate them. Whatever you want to happen for you, do it for someone else. Instead of your staff always being a blessing to you, turn the tables and be a blessing to them, too. Just by simply learning how to say two words, "Thank you," can diffuse the in-house squabbling.

> 1 Thessalonians 5:12-13 (AMP)
> Now also we beseech you, brethren, get to know those who labor among you [recognize them for what they are, acknowledge and appreciate and respect them all] —your leaders who are over you in the Lord and those who warn and kindly reprove and exhort you. And hold

> them in very high and most affectionate esteem in [intelligent and sympathetic] appreciation of their work. Be at peace among yourselves.

Don't suffer from Moses' syndrome. Moses had such compassion for the people that it cost him access to the Promised Land. No matter what, you must be obedient and follow God's instructions. Some of the people who have been entrusted to your care will try to sway or change your mind regarding the directives instructions that are given. They will do that because normally instruction or correction takes them from their comfort zone. Because of Moses' disobedience, he received a punishment. All that he worked for, he was allowed to see the Promised Land, but he or Aaron did not get to enter or reap the benefits of the Promised Land.

> Moses and Aaron walked from the assembled congregation to the Tent of Meeting and threw themselves face down on the ground. And they saw the Glory of God. God spoke to Moses: "Take the staff. Assemble the community, you and your brother Aaron. Speak to that rock that's right in front of them and it will give water. You will bring

water out of the rock for them; congregation and cattle will both drink." Moses took the staff away from God's presence, as commanded. He and Aaron rounded up the whole congregation in front of the rock. Moses spoke: "Listen, rebels! Do we have to bring water out of this rock for you?" With that Moses raised his arm and slammed his staff against the rock—once, twice. Water poured out. Congregation and cattle drank. God said to Moses and Aaron, "Because you didn't trust me, didn't treat me with holy reverence in front of the People of Israel, you two aren't going to lead this company into the land that I am giving them." Numbers 8:6-12 (AMP)

After all of our labor, we cannot afford to allow the complaints, murmurs, or dissatisfaction of people cause us to become castaways, and we end up losing all that we have worked so hard to get. According to an article titled, "Why Moses is Denied the Promised Land", Rabbi Shlomo Riskin explains the fatal flaw in Moses' leadership.

Moses thought that he could broaden the mandate to the envoys but never expected that panic might set in and thwart the entire venture of entry into the Promised Land. He clearly overestimated his people. At that time, however, Moses is not yet punished; he may have misjudged, but a leader cannot be condemned for overestimating his nation. However, now comes the follow-up test. When the people are complaining for water, God tells Moses to take the staff and speak to the rock. The rock symbolizes the Israelite nation, hard and obstinate as a rock. "Speak to it," says God, "and you will extract life-giving and Torah-true waters even from this stubborn nation."

Some things that God is going to instruct you to do might sound strange to your people. They will complain among one another, and some will have the audacity to question whether you have heard from God. Don't allow the complaints of the people to change your attitude toward them or what God has assigned you to do. Whenever the assignment has been handed down from God, leaders are responsible for carrying it out to the letter without no distraction or alteration. If we alter it in any way, we get ourselves in trouble with God. Leaders, whether new or old, must hold onto their convictions and standards and don't allow the actions and attitudes of the people to cause them to develop actions and attitudes that will disqualify them from the promises of God. People will be people, and people will come with baggage, different visions, and a myriad of attitudes. They are with your plan one day, but the next day they might think the assignment is ludicrous. Let that not hinder the vision that has been placed in your heart; fulfill the assignment.

> When God heard what you said, he exploded in anger. He swore, "Not a single person of this evil generation is going to get so much as a look at the good land that I promised to give to your parents. Not one—except for Caleb son of Jephunneh. He'll see it. I'll give him and his descendants the land he walked on because he was all for following God, heart and soul." But I also got it. Because of you God's anger spilled over onto me. He said, "You aren't getting in either. Your assistant, Joshua son of Nun, will go in." Deuteronomy 1:34-37 (MSG)

Even in our frustrations with the ones that God places in our ministry, we can't afford to strike out at them. We must continue to love them. Rabbi Riskin also points out:

> He (Moses) sees a willful band of upstarts and shouts, "listen now you rebels (Deut. 20:10) striking out against the rock—the nation—instead of loving them." This time Moses underestimates his people, refusing to recognize their objective suffering as well as their ability to repent. Now God punishes him, divinely understanding that a shepherd who underestimates his flock, who loses proper love and appreciation for them, cannot continue to lead them.

I recall during a difficult time in our ministry when we experienced a horrendous church split. God attempted to warn us several times from messages, but as the saying goes, we were so close to the forest that we could not see the trees. We had several leaders that walked out on us at the very time that we were getting ready to move to our new facility. We loved and trusted them so much that we overlooked the conspiracy. As ministers, we never experienced anything of this nature before. These were people who just received the oil of the anointing, not lay members. Also, these leaders tried to pull out some lay members. Needless to say, as pastors, we were not happy about the situation, nor did we handle the initial shock well. They lied and conspired against us. It was a tremendous attack against our ministry and a personal attack against us. At the initial shock of the events, we wanted to validate ourselves, but we were counseled by our spiritual leaders that there was no need for us to do so. This was simply a trying of our faith. We had to be still and know that God was God. Do you know how hard it was to be still and quiet when every fiber in our being wanted to retaliate?

I remember one day another fellow Pastor called me. I shared with her what was going on. She didn't pacify me nor did she give in to my crying. She simply told me, "Do not inherit the Moses syndrome."

I realized in addition to Moses that Aaron didn't make it to the Promised Land either. So, both Moses and Aaron were held accountable for completing the assignment. My mind quickly started scanning the ministry of Moses, and his great feats, only to realize he allowed the people to cause his disobedience to the voice of God, thus disqualifying him his right to the Promised Land.

During this time, our spiritual leaders interestingly ministered to us. Over dinner, our spiritual dad told us that we hadn't went through anything. Initially, I was shocked to hear this because my wounds, in my own eyes, were still gaping. I wasn't expecting alcohol to be poured in my wound; I expected a Band-Aid. However, for a wound to heal properly, peroxide or alcohol should be poured to capture and eradicate the infection before a Band-Aid or gauze can be applied. Once the infection is taken care of, then an ointment such as Neosporin must be applied to stop the infection from coming back. This applies in the spiritual realm as well.

Our spiritual dad counseled us to continue to love God's people. Again, this is not what I wanted to hear, but it was indeed what I needed to hear. In my flesh and while I was hurting, I did not want to love any people. I wanted all to hurt as badly as I was hurting, not realizing they were. It was like we were all in grief. So, strong godly counsel was the shot in the arm that we needed that started our healing process. We thought it was a bad hit, but with those who had oversight over our lives and who had already been where we were at the time, our spiritual parents had to give us tough love to encourage us to get back on the helm. We still had an assignment to continue to feed, lead, oversee, and love God's people.

These are a few lessons learned during our time in the ministry. We have overcome many struggles, and have had to go through many processes. Therefore, it is my prayer that in spite of all of the things that leaders have to go through in ministry, I pray each of you will continue to love God's people.

As you get your feet wet in your ministry, relax and have fun. Enjoy the position and let it be a tremendous honor to be trusted for this undertaking. God trusts you and has made you ready, willing, and able to endure this journey.

CHAPTER 4

DOMESTIC LEADERSHIP: RESTORING THE FAMILY FOCUS

> "No matter what you've done for yourself or for humanity, if you can't look back on having given love and attention to your own family, what have you really accomplished?" – Elbert Hubbard

Leadership starts at home. If you can't run your own home successfully, how can you run a ministry successfully? Domestic leadership is a topic that you don't hear discussed in great detail in the church. However, focusing on the family is essential to any thriving ministry. The divorce rate is as high in the church as it is in the world. Adultery is running rampant in the church. Why is this happening? We find that many spiritual leaders are taking care of everyone else; however, the family has been neglected for the sake of the ministry. How can we win the world when we find ourselves losing our families?

Spending quality family time is essential. Our natural children deserve our undivided attention. It is time that spiritual leaders take a step back and take the time to listen to our children. If we don't listen to them, someone else will, and it could be someone to whom we don't want them attached. We need to get to know our children again. Half the time, we don't realize how much our children have grown until they are out of our homes and grown-up. We miss so many valuable years of their lives because we become so engulfed in building a ministry that our family life takes the backseat to everything else.

Leadership should be a priority in our homes. In our homes, it is our primary responsibility to be the priests and priestesses of our homes. We need to instruct our families in the Word of God. As instructed to the children of Israel in the book of Deuteronomy, we must keep God's Word before our spouses and children until it will get in their hearts. There is a great responsibility that is given regarding domestic leadership.

> Write these commandments that I've given you today on your hearts. Get them inside of you and then get them

inside your children. Talk about them wherever you are, sitting at home or walking in the street; talk about them from the time you get up in the morning to when you fall into bed at night. Tie them on your hands and foreheads as a reminder; inscribe them on the doorpost of your homes and on your city gates. (Deuteronomy 6:7, MSG)

It is also vital to have fun as a family. Taking a family outing is not a sin. Pastors, spouses, and children need ample time away from the flock so they can stay properly bonded. Even the pastor and his/her spouse need quiet time away from the children. It is amazing how fast a family can lose touch with one another. The focus must be placed back within the family because if we can't win our families, how can we win those abroad?

It should be a primary goal to avoid divorce and losing our children. God ordained the family, but the enemy is attempting to destroy the family structure. Frankly, he is doing a great job at it because we are so busy building our mega-sanctuaries that their families are being destroyed without their knowledge until it is too late. It has been so sad to see powerful men and women of God succumb to divorce, and function as it is the normal thing to do. Ladies and gentlemen, it is time to win our families back. It is time to recover all.

We find in 1 Samuel 30:8 the men were ready to stone David because their families were taken captive by the Amalekites. The men were so engaged in battle in Ziklag that when they returned home, they realized their families were missing. These men were distraught, and as a result, these men wanted to stone their leader because their families were taken captive. Could these men have fortified their homes any better before they left to assist their leader so that this would not have happened?

> Now when David and his men came home to Ziklag on the third day, they found that the Amalekites had made a raid on the South (the Negeb) and on Ziklag, and had struck Ziklag and burned it with fire, and had taken the women and all who were there, both great and small, captive. They killed no one, but carried them off and went on their way. So David and his men came to the town, and behold, it was burned, and their wives and sons and daughters were taken captive. Then David and the men with him lifted up their voices and wept until they had no more strength to weep. David's two wives also had been

taken captive, Ahinoam the Jezreelitess and Abigail, the widow of Nabal the Carmelite. David was greatly distressed, for the men spoke of stoning him because the souls of them all were bitterly grieved, each man for his sons and daughters. But David encouraged and strengthened himself in the Lord his God. David said to Abiathar the priest, Ahimelech's son, "I pray you, bring me the ephod." And Abiathar brought him the ephod. And David inquired of the Lord, saying, "Shall I pursue this troop? Shall I overtake them?" The Lord answered him, "Pursue, for you shall surely overtake them and without fail recover all." (1 Samuel 30:1-8, AMP)

We find children that get themselves in trouble because the parents are so busy about church business that they neglect family business. Children begin doing things out of the norm sometimes to get attention. Unwanted childhood pregnancies and useless suicides have been the result of parents giving their children the time and attention that is required.

Remember our natural children are as important as our spiritual children. We minister behind God's sacred desk and handle church business, but our children sacrifice as much as we do. We should take the time to honor them as well. We can't lose our children all for the sake of what we label as working for God. Working for God must first start at home.

When Adam (Ish) became a living soul, it was his primary responsibility to tend and guard the Garden of Eden. He had the responsibility of naming all the species (livestock, wild beasts, and all animals in general). When Eve (Ishah) was taken out of Adam's side, it was her primary responsibility to be his helper. She was made so Adam would not be alone, and she could be suitable, adapted, and complement him.

> And the Lord God took the man and put him in the Garden of Eden to tend and guard and keep it. And the Lord God commanded the man, saying, "You may freely eat of every tree of the garden; but of the tree of the knowledge of good and evil and blessing and calamity you shall not eat, for in the day that you eat of it you shall surely die." Now the Lord God said, "It is not good (sufficient, satisfactory) that the man should be alone; I will make him a helper meet (suitable, adapted, complementary) for him." And out of the ground the Lord God formed every [wild] beast and living creature

of the field and every bird of the air and brought them to Adam to see what he would call them; and whatever Adam called every living creature, that was its name. And Adam gave names to all the livestock and to the birds of the air and to every [wild] beast of the field; but for Adam, there was not found a helper meet (suitable, adapted, complementary) for him. (Genesis 2:15-20, AMP)

Domestic leadership is important to the husband and the wife of the family. The husband has a primary responsibility to be the head of the household. It is designed for him to make the best decisions for the family. It is his job to decree the blessings over his children. He should be a disciplinarian and be apt to correct his children as necessary. (Please see I said "correct," not "abuse.") It is not his job to provoke his children to wrath, but he should be the encourager.

As the wife, we must step aside and let our husbands have their rightful place as the priest of the home. Even if we are both working and contributing assets into the home, we should respect him enough to allow him to make the decisions concerning what is best for our families.

From the start of our marriage, my husband has designated me to handle our checkbook and the finances of the family. He recognized I was much better at that than he was. However, I still recognize my place, and I discuss the finances before I spend the finances. When our money is deposited in the bank, I pay bills. I resist the temptation to buy things secretly, knowing they are not in our budget.

Also, children must see their parents loving and respecting one another. Children strive better in an atmosphere that is filled with love and peace. So many children have nervous conditions today simply because their homes are a place of chaos, fussing, and fighting. This is not what God had in mind when he established the family. God blessed Adam and Eve and then told them to "be fruitful, and multiply." (Genesis 1:28) How can we "be fruitful and multiply" when there is so much division in our families? The way our children see us treating one another will be embedded in them, and in turn, they will treat their own families the same way.

As instructed in Titus 2, we are called to be self-controlled, submissive to our husbands, chaste, and keepers at home. If we are not operating in these attributes, through our actions we are causing God's Word to be discredited. In today's society, we see many women that have problems with submission because they feel because they "bring home more bacon", they feel they have the final decision; however, this is against God's Word.

It looks like roles are being reversed. Now we have "stay at home dads" and the moms are going out into the corporate world. There is nothing wrong with women aspiring to be all that God has created them to be, but don't forget your role at home. You may be the CEO and have many people reporting to you and submitting to your authority, however, when you get home, your husband is still the CEO of the household, and you must submit to his authority. There is nothing wrong with being submissive to your husband. It puts the house in the correct order.

> Titus 2:4-5 (AMP)
> So that they will wisely train the young women to be sane and sober of mind (temperate, disciplined) and to love their husbands and their children, To be self-controlled, chaste, homemakers, good-natured (kindhearted), adapting and subordinating themselves to their husbands, that the word of God may not be exposed to reproach (blasphemed or discredited).

Ladies, we are the thermostat of our home. We regulate the temperature in the house. We can't be too hot, but we have to stop being so cold, too. There were times during our earlier years of marriage that I would bring my frustrations home from work, and it seemed as though our household was in confusion the whole night. However, I decided to change the way that I was doing things. I realized it was not fair to bring home the added stress to my husband or children. It was not fair to take out my frustrations on them. We must help our husbands by keeping the stress level down in the home. It should our ultimate goal to flow after the example of the Proverbs 31 woman.

> Her husband is known in the [city's] gates, when he sits among the elders of the land. She makes fine linen garments and leads others to buy them; she delivers to the merchants girdles [or sashes that free one up for service]. Strength and dignity are her clothing and her position is strong and secure; she rejoices over the future [the latter day or time to come, knowing that she and her family are in readiness for it]! She opens her mouth in skillful and godly Wisdom, and on her tongue is the law of kindness [giving counsel and instruction]. She looks well to how things go in her household, and the bread of idleness (gossip, discontent, and self-pity) she will not eat. Her children rise up and

call her blessed (happy, fortunate, and to be envied); and her husband boasts of and praises her, [saying], "Many daughters have done virtuously, nobly, and well [with the strength of character that is steadfast in goodness], but you excel them all." Charm and grace are deceptive, and beauty is vain [because it is not lasting], but a woman who reverently and worshipfully fears the Lord, she shall be praised! (Proverbs 31:23-30, AMP)

We have to take care of our children. Our children are our treasures, and we must treat them that way. They are a reward from God, not an inconvenience.

> Psalm 127:3 (AMP)
> Behold, children are a heritage from the Lord, the fruit of the womb a reward.

We must make sure they are well maintained and fed. I have seen mothers bring their hungry children to the church. Because they are behind schedule, they penalize their children. Thus, their children are unruly and disruptive in the church because they are hungry. It is such a shame.

Due to my family having to travel about an hour and forty minutes one way to church, when my children were small, I ensured that my children had a good breakfast before we left home in the morning. It was a sacrifice for me to get up early to take care of my children, but it was well worth it when I was in service and my children were content because their little stomachs were full. To avoid getting behind schedule, it is advantageous to take care of their other necessities the night before such as getting clothes out, ironing, bathing the children, combing hair, finding lost shoes, and making sure the shoes still fit. We have to take charge because if we don't, our children will.

Children will try their hand to be in charge, but as parents, it is still our responsibility to show who has the authority in the household. Children are also manipulative because they will try to play one parent against the other. The husband and wife must provide a united front when it comes to parenting their children. My husband and I have always had the pact that if our children ask us anything, the first thing we say is, "What did your mother say?" or, "What did your father say?" and then we would agree. If my husband said, "No," I said, "No."

> 1 Timothy 3:4-5 (AMP)
> He must rule his own household well,
> keeping his children under control,

with true dignity, commanding their respect in every way and keeping them respectful. For if a man does not know how to rule his own household, how is he to take care of the church of God?

Home is our first responsibility, and we can't neglect it or pawn it off on someone else. It should not be a burden, but a privilege to take care of those in our immediate and extended families. Whatever your title or assignment may be in the church, your ministry first starts at home. With much patience and hard work, if you manage your household properly, there will be no problem with managing the household of faith.

It is time that we get our households back in order, and that will only be done by establishing and maintaining the proper order: God, husband, wife, and then children.

> "Your family and your love must be cultivated like a garden. Time, effort, and imagination must be summoned constantly to keep any relationship flourishing and growing." -Jim Rohn

CHAPTER 5

THE FRAGRANCE OF THE ANOINTING: IS IT REAL OR A KNOCK-OFF?

Psalm 23:5b
You anoint my head with [a]oil; my [brimming] cup runs over.

W ebster defines "anointing" as "to apply oil, ointment, or a similar substance to; to put oil on during a religious ceremony as a sign of sanctification or consecration; to choose by or as if by divine intervention." When we are anointed by God, we have to realize it is something that is tailored for us. When we covet someone else's anointing or try to do things the way that they do things, we become an imposter. When we tamper into someone else's anointing and try to flow in it, we emanate a knock-off fragrance to the nostrils of God.

The anointing that Jesus received from the woman with the alabaster box prepared his body for burial. The anointing that we receive from God will prepare us for burial as well. As Colossians 3:3 states, "For you have died, and your life is hid with Christ in God." If we are walking in someone else's anointing, we are not dead at all, and our fragrance is not authentic to God or the people around us. People can detect a phony, and God knows if we have the goods or not. The anointing that we have been given is not for us, but it is to bless the Lord. Anything other than His anointing is cheap and ordinary.

The commentary on the Amplified Bible describes the anointing from Psalm 23:5 as:

> It is difficult for those living in a temperate climate to appreciate, but it was customary in hot climates to anoint the body with oil to protect it from excessive perspiration. When mixed with perfume, the oil imparted a delightfully refreshing and invigorating sensation. Athletes anointed their bodies as a matter of course before running a race. As the body, therefore, anointed with oil was refreshed, invigorated, and better fitted for action, so the Lord

would anoint His "sheep" with the Holy Spirit, Whom oil symbolizes, to fit them to engage more freely in His service and run in the way He directs—in heavenly fellowship with Him.

Webster defines "fragrance" as "the state or quality of having a pleasant odor; a sweet or pleasant odor; a scent; a substance, such as a perfume or cologne, designed to emit a pleasant odor." What kind of fragrance are we emitting to God? Is it a sweet-smelling savor or is it an unpleasant odor in the nostrils of our God? If we are wearing an anointing that is not designed for our chemistry, we are emanating a smell back to God that does not smell right to Him.

Are we giving off an imposter fragrance or are we producing the real fragrance of the anointing specifically designed for us? Because of different body chemistry, we cannot all wear the same perfume. An imposter fragrance is cheap and it does not have a pleasant smell. Even though it might smell like the real fragrance, eventually it will be known that it isn't real. Who wants an imposter or something cheap when the real fragrance is available? God is not looking for an imposter. He has made us all originals. We are fearfully and wonderfully made. (Psalm 139:14)

We attempt to shout like someone else, pray like someone else, preach like someone else, and sing like someone else. There are too many copycats in the Body of Christ. Why want something someone else has when God has a customized and tailor-made anointing reserved just for you?

God is looking for genuine worship. When we are worshipping, we are worshipping for a one-man audience. In worship, we are in a position to move God off of His throne on our behalf. When we are worshipping to move the people, we are emitting an imposter anointing. The anointing is not designed to move people. This is merely charisma. However, the anointing is designed to destroy yokes of bondage, and then the glory goes back to God.

When we are servants of the Lord, it should be our primary focus to come before God with clean hands and a clean heart. We can't afford to come before our King with prayerlessness, bitterness, unforgiveness, wrath, malice, backbiting, lying, or fear in our hearts. If we choose to serve God in this way, we are discharging an imposter fragrance before the Lord.

When we are praising, worshipping, and serving our God, we should not be concerned about ourselves or others around us. We cannot allow people that have the attitude of the Pharisees to shut down our assignment to the Lord. Our anointing is to bring glory to our God. Our prayers will release an odor to our God.

> Revelation 5:8 (AMP)
> And when He had taken the scroll, the four living creatures and the twenty-four elders [of the heavenly Sanhedrin] prostrated themselves before the Lamb. Each was holding a harp (lute or guitar), and they had golden bowls full of incense (fragrant spices and gums for burning), which are the prayers of God's people (the saints).

Walking in love emits the fragrance of the anointing. Walking in the fruit of the Spirit emanates the sweet fragrance of the anointing. Walking in things that are not pleasing to God emanates the imposter fragrance. Our scent is important to God. Our yes to the Lord emanates the "signature scent" that the Lord has so graciously applied to our lives.

In an article published by Our Daily Bread entitled, "Signature Scent," Ms. Link says, "The idea of signature scent is not new. God introduced it as part of worship. In the tabernacle, a certain scent was to be associated with the Lord (Exodus 30:34-35). The people were forbidden to use this fragrance for anything but worship. (Exodus 30:37-38)."

> Then the Lord said to Moses, "Take sweet spices—stacte, onycha, and galbanum, sweet spices with pure frankincense, an equal amount of each—and make of them incense, a perfume after the perfumer's art, seasoned with salt and mixed, pure and sacred. You shall beat some of it very small and put some of it before the Testimony in the Tent of Meeting, where I will meet with you; it shall be to you most holy. And the incense which you shall make according to its composition you shall not make for yourselves; it shall be to you holy to the Lord. Whoever makes any like it for perfume shall be cut off from his people." (Exodus 30:34-38, AMP)

Our anointing and fragrance is for God, but under the new covenant, we as Christians have become God's "signature scent" to the world (2 Corinthians 2:14-15). My prayer is that as a Christian, God's signature scent is emanating from my vessel for the world to smell the difference.

When we've been alone with Jesus, there is a difference others know; and to them it's like a fragrance that we leave where'er we go. – Hess

Bibliography

Link, J. A. (2010, March 23). *Signature Scent*. Retrieved March 23, 2010, from RBC Ministries: Our Daily Bread: http://www.rbc.org/devotionals/our-daily-bread/2010/03/23/devotion.aspx

Reid, D. R. (1983/84). Spiritual Leadership. *Devotions for Growing Christians*, Retrieved February 19, 2010, from www.growingchristians.org/dfgc/leader.htm

(2005). *Characteristics of Christian Leadership*. Retrieved February 24, 2010, from 2005 YouthTRAIN:http://www.youthtrain.com/assets/samples/leadership_development/principles_of_christian_leadership.pdf

Reagan, D. (n.d.). *A Servant's Heart–Humility*. Retrieved February 25, 2010, from www.learnthe-bible.org/a-servants-heart-humility.html

Riskin, S. (2002, June 21). Why Moses is Denied the Promised Land? Torah Study. *Jewish News of Greater Phoenix*, Retrieved March 22, 2010, from www.jewishaz.com/jewishnews/020621/torah.shtml

Strong's Concordance
The King James Version Bible
The Message Bible
The Amplified Bible (1987). La Habra, CA: The Lockman Foundation
The Living Bible
Webster's Dictionary

www.ingramcontent.com/pod-product-compliance
Ingram Content Group UK Ltd.
Pitfield, Milton Keynes, MK11 3LW, UK
UKHW041944230426
12048UKWH00008B/119